To Belladonna Tooke –
"May the hair on your feet
grow ever longer" – Tolkien

Elizabeth Betts Ingraham

Dig Weeds,
My Son!

Dig Weeds, My Son!

by Elizabeth Betts Urquhart

The Naylor Company
Book Publishers of the Southwest
San Antonio, Texas

Library of Congress Cataloging in Publication Data
Urquhart, Elizabeth Betts, 1910-
  Dig weeds, my son!
  1. Betts family. 2. Urquhart, Elizabeth Betts, 1910- I. Title.
CS71.B57 1973   929'.2'0973   73-20047
ISBN 0-8111-0518-0

Copyright © 1973 by ELIZABETH BETTS URQUHART

This book or parts thereof may not be reproduced without written permission of the author except for customary privileges extended to the press and other reviewing agencies.

ALL RIGHTS RESERVED

Printed in the United States of America

Dedicated with love

to

my brothers and sisters

Acknowledgments

SPECIAL THANKS to my close and longtime friend and counselor, Dr. Valeria R. Juracsek of Ann Arbor, Michigan who encouraged me in this writing venture and to Katherine Penhale, a good friend, who patiently did the typing of my manuscript.

AT ONE TIME I thought I'd title this sort-of-a-saga of the Reverend W. A. Betts, Sr. family "View from a 1/16." The reason for that is, I quite often thought of myself *as* a 1/16th, especially once when a brother I hadn't seen for twenty-four years kept calling me "sister" instead of Elizabeth. I asked him if he called me that because that's what they called me when I was a baby, or because he couldn't remember my name. He grinned and replied, "Want me to tell you the truth? I can't remember your name!"

The *Dig Weeds, My Son!* comes from the very fact that Papa's whole life seemed based on that idea both literally and figuratively. He was a Methodist preacher and moved from conference to conference, state to state, building up the churches in every way and starting a beautiful fruit and vegetable garden at each parsonage we lived in. "Idle hands are the devil's tools in the devil's workshop." So whenever a boy in the family was discovered doing nothing and Papa came into view, it was *always* "Dig weeds, my son!" Not daring to grumble or mumble, the boys would leave for the garden.

In all areas of his life Papa was a hard taskmaster. We children found this very difficult; and living with him was a riotous, sad, happy, angry, funny, rebellious time rolled into one. All in all he was an interesting person. Born in September, 1857 in Blockersville, North Carolina, son of a

Methodist minister, he grew up, as far as we knew, in the bosom of a *happy* family. Grandpa Betts was reverred by all who knew him. Robert E. Lee called him "that model chaplain." Papa's mother was Elizabeth Davis Betts (for whom I was named). She died when Papa was in his teens and since he worshipped her, it nearly broke his heart. But Grandpa married again and the stepmother became honored and respected by Papa and his brothers and sisters.

We children always heard, "Papa was wild when he was young." We didn't know exactly what was meant, and could only guess. He was very poetic, artistic, had a beautiful basso profundo voice, was an excellent student and was popular with the girls. He went to the University of North Carolina at Chapel Hill, lived in old West Hall, majored in philosophy, started a glee club, was class poet, and graduated in the class of 1880 which, by the way, was the first to graduate after the end of the Civil War. (The university was closed all during the war, of course.) On the night of commencement, Grandpa was seated on the rostrum with the other members of the Board of Trustees and when Papa's name was called to come to get his diploma, Grandpa took it for him. At that moment Papa was on the high seas, on his way to New York City to study YMCA management. When Papa was in his teens he wrote a poem about Grandpa — "Apples of Gold in Pictures of Silver."

APPLES OF GOLD IN PICTURES OF SILVER
Affectionately Dedicated to Papa
by W. A. Betts

A stranger passing on the streets of Frederick, Maryland,
Was marching with a Southern corps, a brave and warlike band.
By chance he saw a sight full pure enough for heaven's dome,
Which made his heart leap forth with joy in tender thought of home.

A little maiden pure and sweet seemed flitting through the air,
Transformed into an angel bright, with brow untouched by care.
Her hand of mercy seized a cup filled with sparkling water,
And poured well full the soldiers' tins, like a queenly daughter.

A vessel near was kept supplied with the refreshing draught,
And as she worked with hands of love, so merrily she laughed.
A chaplain of the "Thirtieth" (this stranger passing by)
Stood rapt, in meditation on the sight which met his eye.

He gazed with fond devotion as his trembling hand he laid
Upon her youthful head and said, "God bless you, little maid!
He will bless you, for he hath said whoever shall e'en give
A cup of water in his name, shall a reward receive."

He went his way, absorbed in thought, when suddenly in rear
He heard a little pit-a-pat upon the sidewalk near.
Facing about he met the maid, who sweetly said:
"Mama says will you please come back there, just a moment, sir?"

She led him through this door and that, through passage, hall and out
Into a parlor, large and bright — garbed in his "roundabout."
A lady rose with queenly grace, who said: "Kind sir, you spoke
Unto my little girl just now, God's blessings to invoke."

The stranger bowed with modest air in assent to the same,
And then with guests and relatives a moment's chat they claim.

The chaplain leaves. He bids adieu to friends collected there
And joins his comrades on the march, the crown to win
and wear.

* * *

The war is o'er. In "Sixty-six," on N.C.'s eastern shore,
Is found an humble Pastor who is weary and footsore.
The ills of war have plied too well their scourge with iron
hand
And Carolina's goodly soil is desolate land.

The Pastor, too, partakes of this misfortune of his state.
Chill penury applies with pain her comfortless ill-fate.
His little ones about him are in almost threadbare clothes;
And other bare necessities the pantry also shows.

We find him on a summer eve engaged in garden work,
Intent that he will persevere, nor e'en one duty shirk.
When lo, a lad calls at the gate! "A letter, sir!" he said.
The Pastor took the missive brought, then broke the seal
and read.

He learned it was from distant friends of Frederick,
Maryland,
And brought glad tidings to his heart, as sent by Mercy's
hand.

His nerves gave way; o'ercome with joy at such outlook for
fate,
He sought a stump which stood nearby — his thoughts to
collocate.

He read that friends, in thoughtful love, their very best
have done,
And that a box of "sundries" have been shipped to
Wilmington.

That night around the household hearth, to our Father's care
These "friends indeed" were wafted up in humble heartfelt prayer.

Bost's Mills, Cabarrus County, N.C., July 14, 1876.

Sometime along the years Papa had met a lovely young college girl whose name was Lillie Wadsworth. She attended and graduated from Columbia Female College in South Carolina. They were married and went to live in Charleston, South Carolina where Papa was superintendent of the YMCA. Not long after that, he decided to enter the Christian ministry. While there, an interesting event occurred. A man showed up at the Y office all disheveled and unshaven, asking for help. Papa gave him ten dollars, told him to go get cleaned up, have a meal and return about 2 P.M., or some stated hour. When the man came back, Papa was out of the office at the moment, so the man took a piece of tablet paper and wrote a little poem, a note of thanks and left. The man was Frank L. Stanton, and fifty years later when Papa was in Atlanta, he went up to Mr. Stanton's office and showed him the yellowed note which he had kept all those years. Tears rolled down Mr. Stanton's cheeks. He embraced Papa and spent the whole day showing him and two of my brothers around the city in his chauffeured limousine. He told Papa how he happened to write "Mighty Lak a Rose." He said his baby was very ill once with a high fever. As he and his wife looked down in the crib at the flushed little face he said, "He looks mighty like a rose, doesn't he?"

Papa and his wife Lillie had six children. Albert Deems was the first. A cute story they tell about him is that when he was about four, Papa taught him that the Negroes were our brothers and sisters in the sight of God. Little Albert spent the next day sitting on a fence post outside the parsonage nodding his head at every Negro who passed and saying, "Good day, colored brother," or "Good day, colored sister!" Years later he graduated from Princeton University and was president of Paine College, Augusta, Georgia. That was a Methodist college for Negroes, and when Albert died several years ago the Methodist Churches of South Carolina started a scholarship fund in his name to benefit students at Paine. Albert's first wife was Katherine Budd of New Jersey. Later he married Evelyn De Medici of South Carolina.

The second child was little Mary. She died in early childhood (from pneumonia, perhaps). Then came Lucy, a bright, black-eyed girl who graduated from Randolph-Macon in Virginia, taught school, then married Herbert Gunter who was a vice-president of Pilot Life Insurance of Greensboro, North Carolina. The fourth child was Daniel Lander (the one I didn't see for twenty-four years). He graduated from Wofford College in South Carolina, taught for a while at Carlisle Military Academy, then left for Brazil as a Methodist missionary. He served in the field for fifty years and was deeply loved by all who knew him. He met and fell in love with his lovely wife, Frances Scott, on the boat on the way to Brazil. She was a missionary too.

Next came Evelyn. She was a pretty, intelligent girl, who graduated from Wesleyan College in Georgia and taught Latin. She married a Baptist minister, Dr. Edwin A. Bell, and after serving pastorates in Wyoming, Colorado and Michigan they went to Europe as church representatives and lived in Paris and Zurich for eighteen years after the end of the second world war. At present they are living in *active* retirement in a beautiful home of their own in Sanford, North Carolina. They tell this story of Evelyn. Papa had family prayers twice a day. This was always *most* boring to the children. Each one had to recite a Bible verse, and a different one each time. The youngest could get away with "Jesus Wept" or "God is Love," but not so the older ones. To liven up the procedure, but not to be *too* sacrilegious, one night Evelyn came out with "Moab is my Wash-pot; over Edom will I cast my shoe!" The rest of the family broke into giggles and Papa even smiled. In later years, at family prayers with Papa, Ann, a grandchild, said, "Blessed are the shoemakers!"

After Evelyn, then came Lil. As Mama often said, "When God made Lillie, he threw away the pattern." Tragically, her mother died when she was born, but when she was two, Papa married again and so she was to have a mother after all. A sweet, lively child, she had a very inquisitive mind, absorbed everything in sight. When she grew up she was extremely creative, sewed, designed clothes, wove, cooked to perfection, flew her own plane, invested in the stock market wisely and travelled to Europe twice. She had studied nursing and graduated from Danville General Hospital in Virginia. She and a classmate decided to venture far from home and got a position in Hurley Hospital, Flint, Michigan. There a fine surgeon asked her to become his office nurse and first assistant in the operating room. This she did for forty years. (When I graduated from nursing school he wrote me a letter of congratulations saying in part, "If you have as much intelligence and ability in your whole body as your sister has in her little finger, you'll go far.") But most of all, Lil gave of *herself*. When I was ten years old she sent me pretty dresses which she made herself. She sent us all toys and many other gifts over the years. When I finished high school she took me completely under her wing and put me through the University of Michigan School of Nursing. To tell about her will fill a book. So I'll say more later. Right now she is retired and lives in a lovely home on the shore of Lake Huron, Harbor Beach, Michigan.

Papa's sister Sally came to keep house for him and the five motherless children. All these years the family had moved from place to place. As I've stated before, Papa would take a year to build up a church and then move on. When he came to the little town of Ninety-Six, South Carolina, he met Lula Frances Young — a girl just two years out of college — twenty-two years old. He was forty-one. She had her A.B. degree and Bachelor of Music from Greenville Women's College, Greenville, South Carolina, which is now part of Furman University. Her father, John Christopher Young, owned 1,500 acres of land in the area, so she was raised in the country. When she was nine years old she was sent to boarding school at the Misses Giles Academy in Greenwood. She had five brothers who adored her, and they really were shocked when she married a preacher with five kids — the oldest just six years younger than she was! However, I think she was a pretty good little mama to the children and during all her lifetime they showed their love for her in many ways.

Mama was a remarkable woman. Of that there is no doubt. Everyone who ever met her loved her. She was sweet and gentle most of the time but could be firm as a rock when the need warranted. Also, she could "fly off the handle" as we called it if we pushed her too far, and we'd run for our lives, laughing as we flew — because we knew she'd never hurt us. Papa, with *all* his cruel sternness with us, the children, was *never* anything but courtly and really loving towards her. I *never* heard her call him by name. It was "Mr. Betts" to outsiders and "Your Papa" to us children. It used to seem magical to me when he *always* knew when she was speaking to him even when he wasn't looking at her when she spoke. We used to say the way he hurt her was by hurting the children. And by that I mean by his severe strictness. The switchings we got were from peach tree switches he kept in a vase on the mantel! It was "Hold out your hand, daughter." And when those steel blue eyes bored through you, Wow! Mama would say, "Oh, children, he doesn't mean any harm. He's just doing what he thinks is best."

The first child to be born of this union was Grace Estelle. Then Virginia Sprott and Sara Pauline. They were the first three — born a year apart. Mama dressed them like triplets, and cute they were from the pictures we have of them. Grace grew up, graduated from Greensboro, North Carolina, Womans' College and married a fine architect, Raleigh James Hughes. Virginia graduated from Andrew College in Georgia and married Rose Lee Fogleman, an officer of the Federal Land Bank. Sara went to Randolph-Macon Institute in Virginia and became a medical record secretary. These three were especially devoted to each other all their lives.

The next two children were Mildred and John. We always spoke of them in hushed tones because they died of separate diseases only six weeks apart. (Mildred was three and John one.) Mama was never one to brood, but I heard her say once with tears in her eyes and her voice breaking, "My arms were never so empty." The children were buried in a cradle grave at Centenary, South Carolina.

Charles was number twelve, I believe, of the sixteen. (Golly! that makes yours truly the thirteenth.) He was a very bright little guy — solid and handsome. A wealthy family in Florida wanted to adopt him saying, "You have so many; please let us have him!" The older children taught him to recite the whole of "Mecca, mecca, parva stella" by the time he was three years old. Mama dressed him in Buster Brown suits with his hair Buster Brown style. I have a picture which I treasure. It is of Charles, about four, with his arm protectingly around me — his two-year-old shy sister.

Papa was president of Montrose College in Mississippi when I was born. The rest of the kids had diphtheria at the time so the doctor isolated Mama and me for several weeks. One or two of the older ones had read a novel they loved where a little sister was born to the family and they called her "little sister." That became my name then and there and most of the family still call me Sis or Sister. To the others and to Papa and Mama it was Elizabeth. But, oh, how I disliked the name. When we'd move to a new town and I had to tell the new teacher that *long* name I nearly died. So when I went away to school I called myself Betty and that's what most folks call me now. After I finished college I married Donald Urquhart, a manufacturer's agent, and we have a fine son, James Betts Urquhart, teaching at Starr Commonwealth, Albion, Michigan. He and his wife Carol have four children: Matthew and Andrew (twins), Cindy and Monica.

Then along came Bill. He was born in White Springs, Florida and was named for Papa — William Archibald Betts, Jr. Many's the time we teased him about that! A sweet smart boy he was — very quiet and "kept his own counsel." I felt very close to him. When we moved to Wichita Falls, Texas I was a bashful, frightened twelve-year-old. Bill and I had to walk about sixteen blocks to school. At recess he was off and playing with the other kids, but just a few minutes before the bell rang for school to "take up again" Bill would saunter over to where I was standing alone in a corner of the school yard. In his hand there would be two Eskimo pies. He'd give me one and he'd eat one, never saying a word. I'll never forget that sweet gesture. He had a quick temper too, though, and one day he was teaching me how to ride a Texas cow pony, named Boss. I kept dropping the reins in my fright. Finally, he yelled, "Ya dam' fool, can't you hang on to 'em?!" And with that he slapped me on the leg with the reins and ole Boss took off down the sandy road with me yelling at the top of my voice. Bill could "cuss up a storm," too. With Papa around none of us dared to even say *darn* or *gee*. Well, one day, Henry, the youngest, and Bill were sawing wood with a crosscut saw. They were quite deep in the forest and didn't have any idea that Papa was anywhere near. Henry began to lie down on the job a little and Bill called him every name in the book and *more*. Papa suddenly appeared behind him and stood quietly listening for a moment. Then he stepped up to Henry, took over his end of the saw, continued sawing and said to Henry, "Go along home, son." Bill said he thought he'd really catch it but Papa didn't say a word. He's now a pediatrician in Tulsa, Oklahoma, and has a beautiful wife, Marie, and three cute daughters, one named for me!

Gladys was born when we lived in Miakka, Florida. That night, we children thought her cry was that of a wildcat! (Those animals were quite prevalent in that part of Florida at the time.) All during Glad's childhood we would torment her with "wildcat!" whenever she would lose her temper even slightly. She was always firm in her belief in her own judgment and is to this day. We were all so in awe of Papa that we didn't "sass" much. But one day I passed the study where Gladys was being punished with the peach tree switch. I heard her say to Papa, "Why don'tcha beat on Henry sometime? You're always beatin' on me!" And once when we lived in a little sheep-ranch town in Texas she accepted an invitation to Sunday dinner from the Browns — dear friends of the family and who lived on a nearby ranch. Now, Papa was adamant in the rule that no one of us was ever to go to Sunday dinner away from home. Gladys took matters into her own hands and after church hopped into the Brown's surrey with Miss Frank — deciding that at least she would have a grand dinner and loads of fun under her belt before the switching she knew she'd get later!

Gladys, by the way, was named Gladys Brown Betts, the Brown being for Mama's music professor, Dr. Wade R. Brown, who later became dean of the School of Music at the University of North Carolina (Greensboro campus) and the auditorium there is named in his honor.

Gladys was sent to The University of Texas through the kindness of our Lil. She was chosen to be one of the "Blue Bonnet Belles" one year there. After graduation she taught a while, then was married to Stuart W. Bradford, of Saginaw, Michigan, who is a fine artist (commercial is his profession, but his paintings have hung in the Detroit Institute of Arts on exhibit).

The caboose of this Betts train was Henry Martin. We always called him Mama's little rotten egg; loved him dearly and easily excused the amount of spoiling Mama did of him. He was a good-looking little rascal —towheaded and brown eyed with a beautiful smile. He was born in Hastings, Florida. Along with the rest of the family, Bill and I were so happy when he arrived and were quite possessive of him. The doctor who delivered him was a Dr. Hewitt. He had a large crooked nose and Bill and I used to call him "Ole Doctor Crooknose." When he came to our home to check on mother and babe he would leave with his satchel in his hand, smirk at Bill and me and say, "Well, I'm taking him back today — have him here in my bag!" We'd go crying upstairs to Mama's room and look in the baby basket which stood on the trunk in the corner — checking to see if we still had him safe and sound.

I remember, too, the nurse, Miss Martin, who took care of Mama and Henry. She used to lecture us children on being careful *never, never* to touch that soft spot on the top of his head, for if we did it would kill him instantly. That boggled our minds! Gladys, who was only a baby herself then, of course, picked up Henry's little finger and nearly bit it off! She'd seen adults lovingly nibble at the baby hands and she thought she was "loving the baby!" A little sibling rivalry there perhaps, but we took it the other way.

Henry was the mimic in the family. He could imitate anything and anybody. We all loved to "talk about Papa" when Papa was gone. Henry, when his voice changed, could manage to make us think Papa had come back to surprise us talking about him! That would scare us silly. He could tease Mama with his imitations too. He might come up behind her and say, "Lula Dear, will you please fix my tie?" Mama would turn around and obediently start to do as he asked — and seeing Heink would burst out laughing and chide, "Oh, Henry!" Once she and Henry were capping strawberries at the kitchen table, Henry's back was to the door. He was having a gay old time mimicking Papa — using pompous, flowery language, interspersing it with "wifey dear." He was going on and on; Mama looked up and saw Papa standing quietly in the doorway, enjoying her discomfiture! Then he grinned at her and said, "Never mind. Let the jackass bray!" Henry's a lawyer in Austin and married to Laurie Simmons, a descendant of Sam Houston.

The last five children were the ones I knew the best. The older ones we rarely saw except once in a great while. They were in college or married, and we felt them to be company when they came to visit. They were wonderful to us, sent us grand Christmas presents, remembered our birthdays, sent us clothes and best of all, loving supportive letters. I remember the year I was twelve I was *dying* for candy which Papa wouldn't let us have because it would "rot our teeth!" I charged about a dollar's worth a month for a few times and Virginia would mail me that dollar every month. She would slip it in a letter to me.

As in most homes, Christmastime was an exciting and warm experience. Papa was especially lenient during that season. He would tell us that Santa Claus was a myth, but would smile tolerantly when we woke up on Christmas morning to find footprints in the ashes of the fireplace which Mama had put there the night before to prove to the little ones that indeed there was a Santa Claus! We always had to have breakfast before we rushed into the room which held the tree, and the excitement and anticipation was heart-pounding! Ecologists today would have a fit, but when we lived in South Carolina our Christmas trees were always holly trees. Papa would go out in the woods and chop one down, and the night before Christmas he and Mama would decorate it after we children had gone to bed. I remember that all the small gifts were tied with red and white ribbon and hung on the tree. The larger gifts lay underneath. Uncles and aunts and older brothers and sisters had sent the many presents in boxes days before, and Mama had hidden them away from the eyes of the children. Oh, yes, and on Christmas day we could eat all the candy we wanted to without Papa saying a word! There was always a Christmas Eve service at the church and afterwards a tree, and Santa Claus passing out bags of hard candies to all the children. I distinctly remember my terrible fright at having Santa pat my head and saying, "Hello, little girl." I screamed bloody murder!

On Christmas night we always had fireworks. The little ones could light sparklers; but Papa shot off the firecrackers and Roman candles. We would stand in a semicircle around him while he put on the show! Sometimes when an older brother was visiting us Papa would invite him to participate.

On every holiday, unless it came on a Sunday or Christmas, our family was invited to spend the day at the home of one of the parishioners. What a wonderful time we would have! We'd get all dressed up early in the morning of the event, and wait on the front porch of the parsonage for the host to drive up in his automobile to take us to his home. It usually was a lovely house in the country with a rope swing under the shady trees and grape arbors with golden, luscious scuppernongs if they were in season, or watermelons to feast on — in their time — and always a scrumptious dinner at noon topped off with homemade freezer ice cream. What a day! Late in the afternoon the host would gather us up in his car and with choruses of thanks we'd ride blissfully happy back to our house and to bed.

All PKs (preachers' kids) of my time — in the South anyway — will remember the Poundings. A few days after we'd move into the Parsonage, on arriving in the little towns, we'd be sitting around the supper table, or having prayers afterwards, perhaps, when there would be a knock at the door. When Papa went to answer it there would be cry of "welcome" from a large group of folks outside; then they would all troop in, bearing many gifts of food, mostly staples, supposedly a pound of this and a pound of that.

Then we'd gather in the living room and a spokesman for the members of the church would give a welcoming speech and maybe several others would talk. Papa would make a gracious thank-you speech and say how glad we were to be in their town. Later the kids and we would go out in the yard and play and get acquainted. These Poundings were a warm and beautiful experience.

New Years Eve there was a "Watch Night" service at the church. Very few people attended, as I remember, but all the Bettses had to be there. We'd pray together, and as the New Year arrived all would sing, "Auld Lang Syne" and "God Be with You 'Til We Meet Again" — then silently and quietly we'd walk slowly back to our homes.

With all the restrictions imposed by Papa, it was strong in the hearts of all the children, I believe, to leave home for good at the earliest possible moment. This feeling was supported by Mama, I think — probably vicariously wishing to be gone herself! Anyway, when I was fifteen, Grace took me to Greensboro where I lived with her a while, and then I went to live with Ross and Virginia. They all (Sara, too) were wonderful to me, and I went to high school there in Greensboro. I spent my summers in Michigan with Lil and Evelyn. The first Christmas the girls decided I might go home for the holidays. It was to be a surprise to Mama and Papa and the three children left at home. I was to take all the presents in my suitcase, and left on the train Christmas Eve. Durham (where I was going) was about forty miles away. When the train rolled into the station, I got off and walked the distance to our house, carrying that heavy suitcase with me. On getting to our house I found it empty! No one in the neighborhood knew where the folks had gone. It was nearly dark and I was standing disconsolately on the sidewalk when a man drove up and asked, "Are you looking for the Bettses? I'll take you to where they live now." I was desperate, so hopped into his car and soon we stopped at another house. Never in my life had I ever been glad to see Papa! But that night I practically fell into his arms! Mama and the kids were so glad to see me and we had a wonderful Christmas together. I've forgotten now why Papa had changed houses, but he was superannuated and that meant we rented our own homes instead of living in a parsonage.

No one ever knew when Papa would make a startling decision about anything. Not even Mama. She'd sometimes say to us, "Children, Papa is hatching something! He was tapping on the head of the bed last night." Sure enough, soon there would be an announcement like, "We're moving to such and such in November" — or whenever. Conference was always in the fall and we knew we'd be moving in November!

It wasn't always a *move* that he was hatching, however. In Olanta, South Carolina, when I was about nine or ten he popped up with, "Elizabeth, I'm taking you to Florence (South Carolina) tomorrow to see a throat specialist." The next day we arrived at the hospital there and a famous surgeon, Dr. McCleod, snatched out my tonsils. I hemorrhaged and had to remain in the hospital several days, longer than expected — away from Mama for the first time in my life, and sick with loneliness for her. When I was finally discharged, we hitched a ride on an ice truck back to our little town. The driver let us off at the crossroads and we walked the rest of the way home (probably three or four blocks). Mama said later that my face was as white as a sheet when I walked in the house.

Papa was a stickler for the truth, but would use it for his ends. Anyway, I heard him ask the surgeon, "Dr. McCleod, do you think Texas would be good for my daughter's health?"

The doctor replied, "Mr. Betts, Texas would be good for anybody's health."

So when we'd been home a few days, Papa sprang the news to Mama that "We're going to Texas for Elizabeth's health!" Now she had always gone docilely on all his other moves until now. "*No*, not that far away." And she stuck by that for a few months. But one day he took Bill and Charles (I think they were about eight and twelve) and went on out to Texas — Wichita Falls, to be exact. He'd gotten the position of preaching on a circuit — one church being a small congregation in the north section of Wichita. He established himself and the boys in the parsonage, did the washing and the cooking himself — bought a cow and some chickens. Once in a while he would take the boys out to a nearby restaurant for a meal. One boy finally brought Mama out with a pitiful letter saying, "Please come. Papa took us out to eat today and they gave us some rotten turnip greens!" Later we knew it was *canned* spinach — a dish they'd never had before.

Mama, Gladys, Henry and I finally started on the three-day and three-night train trip — day coach — to Texas. First, we stopped by Mama's childhood home in Ninety-Six, South Carolina, where her brother Ben and his wife Mattie Mae still lived. We had a grand reunion there with all Mama's kin — then, on to Texas!

These things I remember about that trip:

As we crossed the Mississippi on the train ferry, we were *so* excited! A man asked Henry, who was five, "Haven't you ever crossed the Mississippi before?"

"Oh yes, sir," answered Heink, "once when we were going from South Carolina to Florida!"

Then when we got to New Orleans we had to change trains, so took a bus to the other station across town. There was a layer of heavy fog over the city and the air was full of huge mosquitoes. That was my first and only sight of New Orleans!

When we finally arrived in Wichita Falls we were so happy to see our brothers. Papa was so happy to see Mama that he tried for a while to make us all delighted to be there. He took us on interesting trips around the city, introduced us to many nice people, and even let Gladys

17

and me use an old barn on the premises for a playhouse. He and the boys started a garden of vegetables and the boys learned to milk our cow.

In Wichita Falls they used to have severe "Northers." Many families had storm cellars and we loved the excitement of being invited into a neighbor's cellar whenever a storm seemed imminent.

Also, in our new parsonage we had electric lights, a gas stove, and gas logs in the fireplace. Real big city stuff!

When Papa was out of the house we would really raise Cain. Mama was very sympathetic and understood our need for that safety valve for our emotions, but sometimes it got a "little much" for her. Once, on her birthday, Papa was out of town and we said, "Now, Mama, you stay in bed this morning and let us fix breakfast for you." We served in style, I can tell you. We decorated the house with garlands of colored tissue paper, covering the light bulbs to give a rosy glow to the dining room. (Imagine *red lights* in a parsonage!) We fixed our favorite breakfast, not the usual hot oatmeal, etc., but melted cheese on toast and cocoa with marshmallows. When we finally called Mama to the table and were gazing at her fondly, she looked around at each of us and said, "Children, do you know what I want most for my birthday today? A little peace and quiet!" I hope we complied!

In whatever town we lived, the people there quickly realized what a rigid strict atmosphere we were being raised in, and they cooperated one hundred percent in helping us do the fun but innocent things when Papa was absent. We would spread out in all directions the minute he left town and as soon as anybody would catch sight of his returning, word would reach us. "Your Papa came in on the noon train — get home." And home we'd fly and Mama would breathe easy again because we got there before he did. In one little Texas town the local theatre owners allowed preachers' kids in free to the Saturday matinees. If Papa were preaching in a nearby town, we'd slip in to the cowboy show. The next Sunday he might very well be in his local pulpit — speaking of the "evils of the picture shows." Nobody ever told on us.

He didn't want me to use lipstick or rouge when I was a teen-ager. Mama knew I wanted to be like the other average girls so she allowed me to carry a compact and use it after I got to school. Well, one hot sunny day I'd fixed my face in my bedroom and leaped past Papa's study door, out onto the sidewalk, but holding my parasol to hide my face. I heard, "Elizabeth, come here!"

I said, "I'm late, Papa," and held my parasol even closer.

"Come back here, daughter!"

So back I went and I got a lecture about wearing makeup.

"If all the women of the underworld didn't smear that stuff on their faces I wouldn't care if you did. But I won't have you looking like them. Go wash it off." So, in tears, I did just that.

Papa wanted his children to be protected from all worldly influences and his whole life seemed to be dedicated to that purpose. *Purity* was his theme. Once in his youth he wrote

> Brush from the grape the misty blue,
> Shake from the rose the tremulous dew
> And you mar forever a life.

And a poem by Kingsley that he used to quote often to his daughters was, in part,

> Be good, sweet maid
> And let who will be clever.
> Do noble things —
> Not dream them all day long.

In this day of four-letter words being used quite openly, it doesn't seem in too poor taste for me to tell this story.

Papa kept track of our toilet habits and would ask each day, "Did you have an *action*?" Well, when in church we sang "Oh Happy Day" in which one verse went, "Tis done, the great transaction's done" and we children would shake the pew with our smothered giggles and Mama would bite her bottom lip and shake her head at us. We could see she was having to control her laughter too.

A lady in the congregation once in Texas always sang loudly and with a quivery voice, "Terling On" instead of "Toiling On." Somehow or other, Henry began calling going to the bathroom as "I've gotta go to the Terling On!" We called it that for a long time afterwards.

When Henry was a very little fellow, probably three, he frequently wet the bed. Papa got up at night to "put him on the pot." He finally got a little tired of this and delegated the job to Charles who must have been eleven or twelve. Papa told Charles to set the alarm clock for a certain time and get Henry up. Well, he soon got tired of the arrangement too, and lawyerlike hit upon an idea to take care of the problem and he *and* Henry could get a good night's sleep. He got a string and tied off Henry's little uncircumcised foreskin! In the middle of the night there were blood-curdling screams. Papa rushed in and with scissors cut the string; and I suspect ole Charles got a switching with the peach tree switch!

Mama and all we children had always to sit in the front pew of the church so Papa could keep an eye on us — and believe me, we took up a whole pew! One Sunday morning little Grace was acting up and Papa had her come up and sit in the pulpit. It was Communion Day and the wine and bread were placed somewhere behind Papa. Somehow, unbeknown to the congregation and to him, she got hold of the wine (just *grape juice*) and drank it all up!

The ladies of the church once had Virginia give a recitation before a meeting of the anti-saloon league. She was seven or eight years old and a very independent little cuss.

Papa and Mama were unaware that she had the poem to memorize so they were as surprised and as tickled as the ladies when she rose on cue and said at the end of each verse:

But *I'm* a *Tee — toe — tailer*!

Lillie was chosen to give the children's speech at the Missionary Society meeting which was to raise money for the ongoing work abroad. She was just four and tiny for her age so the ladies stood her on a chair to recite her poem:

I'm *only* four years old,
Yet I'm old enough to say
If we truly love our Savior
His words we will obey.

At this stage she pointed a finger in the direction of a bald-headed man in the front row and exclaimed excitedly, "There's a fly on that man's head!" and continued earnestly:

All cannot cross the ocean.
Our work right here is found.
So, I'd like to ask the children
To pass the hat around!

Dan came home for a visit once while we were living in Florida. He had a lively sense of humor and he taught me (they say) a parody on a religious song, the stanza beginning

Oh, you ought to be a lover of the Lord
If you want to go to heaven when you die.

The parody went

Oh you ought to be the lover of the landlady's daughter
If you want to get the biggest piece of pie!

At prayers that night Papa asked me to choose the song for the service. I sang out the parody — lisping it, I guess, as I was only three years old.

About that same time, Albert visited us. He was telling about climbing into the upper berth of the pullman on his trip home. We had always travelled day coach so I'd never seen a berth. I rushed upstairs where Mama was taking care of the new baby and told her, "Albert slept in the hat rack last night!"

When we moved from Florida to Olanta, South Carolina, I was five years old. We lived there five years and many memories remain with me. I experienced the death of a friend for the first time. She was my next door playmate, Victoria, and died of dysentery. Her mother led me into her room to see her "laid out" and I remember seeing that white-faced child, copper pennies on her eyelids — beautiful white organdy dress on, lying upon a mosquito-netting-covered, four-poster bed. And I remember the sickening sweet smell of cape jessamine that permeated the air of the room.

We lived just a few blocks from the main street of Olanta, but we were never allowed to go to town unless we were dressed up — at least, neatly dressed. One day I was building what I thought was a playhouse. It was really an old garage and I wanted to divide the large doorway in two. So, I decided to nail a narrow plank to the top of the door and have it reach to the ground, thus making two doorways. I asked Henry, who was about four years old, (I was nine or ten) to hold the plank while I nailed it, using the back of the ax for a hammer. Well, the first whack slid down the plank, grazed Henry's head, and the bleeding started! I screamed for Mama; she grabbed Henry and told me to go for the doctor. Barefooted and wild with fear and horror, I stretched my long legs and took off for the doctor's office. It was at the top of a flight of stairs over a drugstore. I rushed into his office and yelled, "Dr. Moore, come quick — I've hit Henry in the head with the ax!"

He said, "Wait a minute, Elizabeth, and you can ride with me!" He had a Model T and ordinarily I would have been thrilled to ride in it but that day I didn't even answer him and was home before he got there.

When Dr. Moore came another time to vaccinate all of us against smallpox I hid and they couldn't find me. So I had mine done by special appointment. Once, too, when I had a loose tooth Papa took me over to Dr. Moore's house while he was working in his garden. He just pulled a pair of pliers out of his pocket and pulled the tooth on the spot. He was a kind, loving old family doctor and a good friend of our family for sure.

It was in Olanta where I first read *David Copperfield*. Papa had a huge library but nothing interesting to a ten-year-old. So in desperation one day I took down *David Copperfield* from the shelf and was thrilled by it. I vowed to name my first boy David and I loved Dora.

We children were always so happy when Papa wasn't home that I sometimes wonder if he ever realized it. He never acted as if he did, but not long ago I ran across a poem among his keepsakes that went like this:

DO THEY MISS ME AT HOME?
By S. M. Grannis
Copyright by Oliver Ditson, Co.

Do they miss me at home? Do they miss me?
'Twould be an assurance most dear
To know that this moment some loved one
Were saying "I wish he were here."
To feel that the group at the fireside
Were thinking of me as I roam. . . .

Oh, yes, 'twould be joy beyond measure
To know that they missed me at home.

When twilight approaches, the season
That ever is sacred to song,
Does someone repeat my name over,
And sigh that I tarry so long?
And is there a chord in the music
That's missed when my voice is away . . .
And a chord in each heart that awaketh
Regret at my wearisome stay?

Do they set me a chair at the table
When ev'ning's home pleasures are nigh,
When the candles are lit in the parlor
And stars in the calm azure sky?
And when the "goodnights" are repeated
And all lay them down to their sleep,
Do they think of the absent and waft me
A whispered "goodnight" while they weep?

Do they miss me at home — do they miss me
At morning, at noon or at night?
And lingers one gloomy shade round them
That only my presence can light?
Are joys less invitingly welcome
And pleasures less hale than before . . .
Because one is missed from the circle . . .
Because I am with them no more?

Very sad if he knew how we really felt. But we just couldn't help it! He was so very strict and so uncompromising.
Now, with Mama, it was an entirely different story. With her gentle, loving ways she was perfection to all her children and was to her dying day.
Grace's daughter, Margaret Lula (Margie Lu), wrote

this lovely tribute to Mama a year or so before Mama left this old earth. I'd like to let you read it now. She called it —

THE CHINA DOLL

A nurse at the nursing home where Grandmother is a patient said to me, "I take good care of your grandmother. She's my little china doll." And, indeed, she does look like a little china doll with the pink bow in her soft, fluffy, white hair, her pink rosebud gown and robe. Even her perpetual sweet smile would look at home on the face of an old-fashioned doll. At first glance you might think, "Now here's a lady who has sat on a cushion, sewed a fine seam and eaten strawberries and cream all her life." You might feel that at her age of eighty-five her only thought is for her own physical comfort, and that the only thing she looks forward to is for visiting hours to begin.

But nothing could be farther from the truth. Grandmother's childhood and young girlhood might have been considered of the strawberry and cream type, but while she was a piano major, preparing for a career as a concert pianist or music teacher, she met a minister who was a widower with five children. They were soon married and eventually had ten children of their own. Grandpa was an individual in his own right and laid down very strict rules for his family to live by. All the children and the many obligations of a minister's wife left Grandmother very little time for her music. She was organist at Grandpa's churches during their early married years, but she soon gave this up and as far as I know, never touched the keyboard again. Her musical talent was pushed aside by the needs of her large family. There must have been times when she longed to sit down and play the piano, but no one ever heard her express any regrets. Instead, she continued to enjoy good music as a listener, and today she urges each grandchild and great-grandchild to learn to play at least one instrument, and she keeps up with their progress with keen interest.

Grandpa felt he must move to a new church each year. They lived in many towns in most of the southeastern states during those early years. Moving such a large family so often would have been enough to wear most people out for several months at a time, but Grandmother took it in her stride. Each parsonage they left was immaculate for the next minister; and the next parsonage was cleaned from top to bottom before Grandmother would permit even one suitcase to go in. Each town they lived in was grateful to have Grandmother with them, even if it was for only a year. For sure her family could not diminish the keen interest and active help given to each neighbor and parishioner.

Those years of child raising were full of the financial problems and hard work you would expect for a minister's family. Those years were deeply saddened for Grandmother by the death of two of her precious babies, within six weeks of each other. But her sadness and severe asthma she developed did not keep her from going on with her busy life.

Love of God, desire for education and good moral standards were the main ingredients Grandmother stirred into each of her children's lives. She must be proud that each one attended college and most of them went on to become lawyers, ministers, missionaries, nurses and doctors and teachers.

Soon after the last child left home, Grandpa's health began to fail. He had led a tremendously active life and he considered his poor health an inconvenient burden to himself! His last illness was a long one and it was both physically and emotionally hard on Grandmother, for he would allow no one to care for him except his "wifey dear." Her patient and loving heart brought her through this phase of life too.

After Grandfather's death she moved to another city where three of her daughters lived with their families. At first she lived in an apartment by herself where she continued to keep up with all the children and their families. She had not had a chance to take the psychologist's advice and develop a hobby to see her through her golden years. And an almost complete loss of hearing and an inability to adjust to any hearing aid soon deprived her of her enjoyment of attending concerts and listening to music at home by records and radio. Several years later, a series of operations and generally declining health persuaded her to move into a daughter's home. After a broken hip required continuous nursing care, she moved to a nursing home. No self-pity shows in her warm heart, even now. The only thing to bring tears to her eyes is worry over a grandchild who was in the Congo during the recent crisis, or the illness of a great-grandchild. But, in each case, her faith never permits her to think that everything will turn out other than all right.

She is proud of each great-grandchild's good grades in school and, at the same time, is full of encouragement when the grades are not as good as they should be. She is full of understanding for the young people today and never wonders "What *is* this younger generation coming to?" The old days are sometimes discussed for the entertainment of family or friend, but Grandmother's thoughts and interests are more often on the space program, the current elections, foreign affairs and everything any member of her family is involved in.

She has found many new friends in the nursing home. If either of the other two ladies in her room is especially sick, Grandmother will be awake off and on all night so she can be sure to call the nurse if help is needed.

Cataracts keep her from reading much, but she still reads her large-print Bible every day and one of her daughters says evening prayers with her. Everybody also wonders about the terrible chaos the world is in, but Grandmother is sure that God will bring us through it all!

She may indeed look like a china doll, but Grandmother has the warm heart and depth of understanding that a china doll can never have.

So that's Margie's dear tribute to our mother, and her beloved grandmother.

Many times I had wondered how on earth Mama had been such a fine pianist and so could give up playing entirely. I questioned her about it on several occasions. She would shrug her shoulders and reply, "Where would I find the time even if we had a piano?" After Papa died and she was living in the apartment all alone, there was a piano among the furnishings. As far as I know, she never touched it. I kept urging her just to try. She grinned and said, "If I knew not a soul would hear me, I believe I might, but in this apartment there are other folks."

I would ask, "Mama, what was the name of your recital piece when you got your degree?"

"I don't even remember — if you can believe that — because I have pushed those days right out of my mind!"

Stubborn that I am, I wouldn't let it drop. Her music professor, Dr. Wade R. Brown, was still alive and residing in Florida. (Mama was in her seventies at this time and he in his eighties.) I wrote him a letter, asking if he remembered her recital music. I still have his answering letter. It read, "I am sure it was Mozart's D Minor Concerto." You see, Mama was one of his most promising students and he remembered her well from those early days. When I received this information I told my husband about it and he did a very sweet thing. He bought a recording of the piano concerto played by José Iturbi and we mailed it down to Grace with whom Mama was living by then. It was to be a birthday surprise. The way Grace told us what happened was this: Mama had gone to church with Virginia, Sara and Bob and Margie and their children. When they returned home Grace had the record player turned on and ready to go. As the group entered the door, the music began. Mama went for the nearest chair and, with tears coursing down her cheeks, said wonderingly, "That's my recital piece!" She hadn't heard it in over fifty years.

Mama had such a big heart and her arms could

enfold all of those who needed to be loved. When I was growing up, my girl friends often would say, "Gee, but I wish I had a Mom like yours!" Firm, indeed, when necessary, but oh, what a gay and free person when it was the right time to be so! The medical folks now believe that one shouldn't prolong life when it's obvious that the patient is suffering, and extreme measures are needed to keep the patient alive. It was that way when Mama was dying, at the age of eighty-eight. Virginia and Gladys and Virginia's son, Dr. R. S. Fogleman, Jr., were with her in the hospital room. She was conscious almost to the last and when she moaned, "Give me back my arms!" the family told the doctors to remove the IV's and let her go in peace! Well, she has her arms now and I just imagine she is using them as she always did: loving those who need love.

And now, to get back to the subject of Papa:

He was a man of small stature — about five feet six, I think. Wiry, quick, and very strong and healthy. I don't recall his ever being sick while I was living at home. He worked hard in the gardens along with the boys. He did a lot of studying, typing, visiting church people, and doing all those things that go along with being a minister. He walked miles every day and ate three square meals a day heartily. He used to follow the pattern of John Wesley; he went to bed at 9:00 P.M., and rose at 5:00 A.M.

Although he was such a small man, his powerful personality overwhelmed most of his children, I believe. And when he was in the house I, for one, anyway, was never afraid of outside harm coming to us! No robber would dare break into our house with Papa there! But when he was away, I was scared pink. One particular night, when we were living in Bamberg, South Carolina in a house Albert bought for us and which Papa named "Hillcrest," he was gone overnight and Gladys and I were afraid to sleep in our bedroom which was far away from the others. So Mama told Bill to put up an army cot and sleep in the room with us. Remember now, Bill was the cussing one of the family! He grumbled, but moved in with Gladys and me. None of us three got much sleep that night because every time Bill thought we girls were asleep he would try to sneak out of the room to get back to his own comfortable bed. Gladys and I would rise up as one and whisper fiercely: "Bill you get back there!"

And he would say, "Blankity — Blank! You dumb so-and-so's!" But he stayed until daylight and we weren't afraid anymore.

The girls in the family were not allowed to date until they were eighteen. One evening, when we lived in the little house on Rainbow Street in Olanta, South Carolina, Virginia, who was eighteen, and Sara who was only seventeen, were sitting with their boyfriends in the two porch swings which faced each other. The porch was screened with velvet bean vines. The night was moonlit, and Papa was out of town! All of a sudden, Virginia warned Sara, "There's Papa coming down the sidewalk!" Sara's date jumped over the railing and hid in the vines until he heard Papa walk up on the porch, speak cordially to Virginia and her boyfriend, turn to Sara asking, "What are you doing out here, daughter? You'd better come along inside." At that, Buddy took off for safer regions!

In his whole life Papa owned but one car. That was about 1913, believe it or not, and it was a Cadillac, given to him by a parishioner. We lived in Florida at the time. I remember the horn went "ah — oo — goo!" And for some reason or other Papa called the car "the gopher." On the beach at New Smyrna one day, Mama and some of the others were sitting on the porch of our cottage and I happened to see Papa driving up the sandy road and ran to meet him. As the car approached me, he tried to stop, but I stumbled in the deep sand and the car ran completely over me! It didn't touch my body at all, but some black grease from the axle dropped on my knee and I thought I was killed! Mama said Papa's face got as white as a sheet — and he said he'd never forget the awful fear that clutched at his heart. I just recall the fuss that was made over me as the grease was carefully washed off my knee! But we talked about it for years afterwards — about "the time Papa ran over Elizabeth with the car!"

Another time, the whole family was going to Sarasota and the car got stuck in deep sand and a man brought a team of oxen to pull us out. While we waited for help to come along we were nearly eaten up by mosquitoes and Papa cut some fans from the nearby palmetto trees to brush them away.

My first experience going swimming happened in Florida too. Papa, Virginia, Sara and I hopped a ride with the mailman in his buggy and went to Venice where we went swimming in the Gulf. At one point Papa swam out to deep water, and unknown to him, I followed. Virginia or Sara yelled and he turned around and hauled me out.

In White Springs, where Bill was born, sparks from a bakery on a hill across town flew over to the street where we lived. It set some houses afire. I had measles, complicated with pneumonia, at the time and Papa didn't want me exposed to the weather, so he made Mama stay inside with me and he got up on the roof and had men pass buckets of water up to him and doused any flame that started there. Some of the other houses burnt but ours didn't.

Grace was down in Florida not long ago (this is 1973) and visited several of the towns we lived in. She said she saw Mr. _____ who used to tease me with, "Here comes Elizabeth — sweatin' on her nose!" In the summertime little beads of perspiration would always pop out on my nose and it always tickled that man to get my reaction when he would call attention to it. I would be furious and would glare at him.

In May, 1910, Papa decided he would go to California and look around to see if he'd like to live out there. It was also the year of Halley's Comet — and incidentally, the year I was born.

He stayed several weeks out there and had many interesting and unusual experiences. He always called on the Methodist minister wherever he went. In San Diego, he noticed on the billboard outside the church that the minister there was "Rev. Will A. Betts." He rang the doorbell of the parsonage and a man who could have easily passed for his double answered. They spent an hour or so together talking genealogy and found that years ago, when England would allow only three brothers to migrate at once, their ancestors were two of the three Betts who came to America. That man's was the one who settled in New York State and Papa's in the Isle of Wight, County of Virginia.

I think it was in San Diego where Papa visited the beautiful gardens built by a big beer king. I remember how impressed he was with the gorgeous labyrinth of roses there. As he left the garden, he remarked to a couple of transients who were seated on a bench at the entrance, "I have spent an hour in Paradise, even though the devil did build it!"

One of the men said, *sotto voce* — "Thar goes a preacher!"

An enterprising restauranteur fixed up the interior of a cave so diners could watch the comet as they were having their meal. Doesn't that sound Hollywoodish? And in 1910 Hollywood was just beginning.

One of Papa's many interests was astronomy and he was thrilled to visit the Mt. Wilson Observatory while he was out there in California. When we were children he would take us out in the yard on clear nights and teach us the names of many of the constellations. I remember once his telling us of the time when he was a lad and his father asked him to climb down in a deep well and clean out the leaves that had drifted in. He happened to look up into the bright daylight and suddenly shouted in awe, "Oh, Father, I can see the stars!"

Music was very important in his and Mama's lives and

they instilled the love of it in us. We sang a lot in our home. Papa taught us to read notes and to sing various parts. When the last five of us remained at home, he taught Charles bass, me alto, Bill tenor and Henry and Gladys soprano (until Heink's voice changed, and then he sang tenor or bass). We learned songs that I have never seen in print or heard anywhere else. They were all religious ones, of course, and I don't know where he got them.

One favorite was "Home of the Beautiful":

> In the realms of bliss eternal, there's a home of love;
> Home of beauty, grand, supernal, glorious home above.
>
> *Chorus*
>
> Home of the beautiful, home of the beautiful,
> Home of the lovely and fair. When shall I see thee, Oh!
> When shall I see thee, Thou home of the lovely and fair?
> Home, home of beauty, Home, home of love;
> When shall I see thee, Home, home above.
>
> Here on earth a pilgrim stranger, wearily I roam.
> Pressing on through toil and danger to my glorious home.
>
> With the storms of life surrounded, mid the ocean's roar,
> Faith looks up to joys unbounded, on the other shore.
>
> In the path of Christian duty, Let me journey on;
> 'Til that home of love and beauty on my vision dawn.

Another:

> There's a land of pure delight, where saints immortal reign;
> Infinite day excludes the night, and pleasures banish pain;
> There everlasting spring abides and never withering flowers;
> Death, like a narrow sea divides this heavenly land from ours.
> Sweet fields beyond the swelling flood stand dressed in living green;
> So to the Jews old Cannan stood, while Jordan rolled between.
> Could we but climb where Moses stood
> And view the landscape o'er, Not Jordan's stream
> Nor death's cold flood
> Should right us from the shore.

Another:

> There is a happy land, not far away
> Where saints in glory stand bright, bright as day!
> Oh, how they sweetly sing — worthy is our Savior King!
> Loud let His praises ring. Praise, praise for aye!
>
> Bright in that happy land beams every eye;
> Kept by a Father's hand, love cannot die.
> Oh, we shall happy be, when from sin and sorrow free.
> Lord, we shall dwell with Thee, Blest, blest for aye.
>
> Come to that happy land. Come, come away.
> Why will ye, doubting stand? Why still delay?

> Oh, then to glory run. Be a crown and Kingdom won,
> And bright above the sun, we'll reign for aye!

The theme of the religionists of that day and age seemed to be "Dig weeds here on earth and receive the great benefits in the world to come." Papa certainly seemed to practice that philosophy, and yet he was very very much concerned with the inventions and discoveries and happenings of things around him as long as he lived. And when he was dying and one of the ministers visiting his bedside started to pray for his soul, Papa said strongly, "Pray for me to live, Brother!" He had lived eighty-eight years then!

The whole family loved music, but Papa wouldn't allow us to sing or listen to "pop music." Therefore we children went to it like metal to a magnet, and quickly learned the hillbilly tunes of the times, and the sad-sack songs like:

> Little Mary Fagan went to town one day
> She went to the pencil factory to
> Get her last week's pay.

And then it went to tell of the horrible things that happened to her as she entered the plant and was murdered by a crazy man! It was terrifying because it had really happened. But Papa didn't want us listening to that trash.

"The Dying Cowboy" was another that we learned and "Hand Me Down My Bottle of Corn" was another.

Chautauqua and Lyceum circuits always visited our little towns and we were frequently taken to those, thank goodness, and therefore got *some* cultural advantages even though against our will. Like many children probably still do, we'd go about for days imitating the opera singers with our quivery voices. Papa didn't ever hear us though.

I remember one time he took a dish of beautiful strawberries he had grown back stage to a visiting prima donna. She was so pleased, and I imagine he presented them with a courtly speech. That was his way.

We children really loved to sing in harmony and would "make the welkin ring" when we were in our own home. But just let Papa take us out to visit some old folks' home and we'd "clam up" on him and just mumble the words! He must have felt like tearing his hair, but there wasn't much he could do about it. We'd pretend we got stage fright.

The girls didn't have to work in the garden. Mama just wouldn't allow it. But once in a while he would take advantage of her being absent for an hour or so and he'd put us to such things as pulling peanuts off the vine or cutting the runners off the strawberry plants.

Once he decided to teach Gladys not to exaggerate. She said, "Can't I stop now, Papa? I've pulled off about a thousand."

He said, "If that's so, daughter, count them." And she did.

He really was a genius at gardening. The boys said, "Sure — with our slave work!" In Cherokee, Texas, Mama said the boys used to look like convicts out there in the garden using pickaxes to drive holes through the rocky ground to plant fruit trees. The ground was dry that year we lived there and when Papa planted several hundred onions, he had the boys dig small ditches between each row, turning the corners at each end and then daily they would place a hose at the start of the ditch and water pumped by the windmill would circulate freely up and down the rows.

We had some beautiful peach trees there, I remember, and that year (about 1923) the locusts came and in an instant, it seemed, had stripped the trees of their leaves and they fell in heaps beneath the trunks and died.

A few years ago my husband and son and I visited

Charles and Henry in Austin. On the way back home we passed so close to Cherokee that my husband said, "Would you like to see the town again?" It had been at least forty years since we'd lived there and I had dearly loved it. Well, as we got there we stopped at a small garage and filling station and went in. Three or four men were standing around talking and I went up to the oldest and asked if he'd lived there long.

"Nope, so-and-so here has!"

I asked "so-and-so," "Do you remember the Preacher Betts' family?"

He said, "Sure I do, and you're Elizabeth. We were in the same grade!" He then told me about everybody and we went over to the church and the parsonage and neither had changed much.

When I went to school there I belonged to a quartette and we called ourselves "The Gypsy Trail Quartette" because "The Gypsy Trail" was our favorite piece of music. We sang at several functions around town and once were invited to go with our wonderful Superintendent of Schools, Mr. Allison, to Ft. Worth to sing over the radio! But Papa wouldn't let me go and I don't believe the other girls went without me. I still have the letter of recommendation that Mr. Allison wrote for me when he knew I was going to a new school.

One Sunday when Papa was preaching there in the little church in Cherokee, some ranchers were driving hundreds of sheep through the town and the baa-ing was so loud Papa had to stop the sermon until they were past!

From Cherokee we moved to Alice. I think we took the train from Llano or San Saba. Anyway, when the conductor took our tickets he said, "Are you Indians?" I guess that Charles and I with our straight black hair, dark eyes and high cheekbones and coming from Cherokee made him think that.

I loved living in Alice too. I got my first kiss from a boy there! On the cheek, but a great, great thrill. The girls there were just so nice and friendly and I felt like one of the crowd. I'd go to the afternoon football games and basketball too. Some of the school yells were:

> Bust a bronco — Beat a bully!
> Root and toot and cut and shoot!
> And we're the gang that
> Does the rootin'
> Zip!
> Bang!
> Alice! ! !

And:

> Slap 'em in the face!
> Kick 'em in the jaw!
> Send 'em to the cemetery!
> Rah — Rah — Rah!

Weren't we awful?

It was in Alice that Bill was called upon at the last minute to recite the Gettysburg Address at some kind of county contest. The boy who was supposed to do it had suddenly become ill. Bill was about eleven but small for his age. As he got up before the judges and the assembled crowd he began with firmness: "Four score and seven years ago — four score and seven years ago — four score and . . ."

One of the judges stood aside and said, "Son, we're going to give you ten points for your school because you were brave enough to try under these difficult conditions!" And Bill sat down, red-faced, but grinning, at the applause.

Charles and I were both on the debating team that year. The subject: "Whether or not the United States should join the League of Nations." Charles was affirmative and I negative. His team won and went on to debate over the state and even before Governor Neff. I think that was what decided Charles to become a lawyer and for years he has been a judge of District Court in Austin. He and his lovely wife, the former Eula Lea Kohn, live there still.

Whenever we moved to a new town Papa was asked to speak at the chapel services which were always held in every school the first hour of the day. Every time he would start his talk by saying, "And I have some little jewels going to this school now!" We would cringe in our seats because we knew that on the playground at recess some kid would ask, "What are you? The diamond or ruby?!"

From Alice we moved to Bamberg, South Carolina, then to Durham, North Carolina. From there I went to live with my sisters in Greensboro, North Carolina. But the family kept on moving! You wouldn't believe how many places.

When they lived at Kitty Hawk, North Carolina, Papa had several little churches in the Outer Banks as it is called, and the folks named him Shepherd of the Banks. I visited them there once, and it was there that I got my first proposal of marriage. I was sixteen at the time and was thrilled beyond belief! The man was ten years older, very handsome, and a college graduate. He said "If you'll stay here and marry me I'll put Bill through medical school."

Later, ole Bill said, "Ya nut! Why didn't you take him up on it?!" (He later became a pediatrician on his own.) However charmed I was by the proposal, I knew I was too young and had high school and college to finish.

When Lindbergh flew the ocean, Papa wanted to put up the memorial to the Wright brothers to help commemorate them at the time of Lindbergh's flight. He wanted it to be on the spot where the plane was constructed, and that was in the front yard of the house that later became the parsonage and where our family lived. The parsonage burned (May 2, 1928) a few days before the unveiling ceremonies but the little obelisk of gray Vermont marble with a crack at its base (caused by the fire) still stands and can be seen by anyone who bothers to enter the little village of Kitty Hawk — near the huge memorial on Kill Devil Hill built by the federal government quite a while later. The cornerstone for that *big* monument was laid on December 17, 1928, twenty-five years since the first flight by the Wright brothers.

The inscription on the small marker states: "On this spot, Sept. 17, 1900, Wilbur Wright began the assembly of the Wright Brothers' first experimental glider which led to man's conquest of the air — Erected by citizens of Kitty Hawk 1928."

I think the reason the parsonage burnt was that Papa was burning some high grass nearby — trying to "pretty up" the place for the celebration. Anyway, the fire destroyed everything the family owned — all Papa's very valuable books — hundreds of them, and some very, very old first editions. Mama lost a trunk full of sheets of music which she had saved all those years, and several other treasures, like the beautiful mother-of-pearl fan that Uncle John had brought her from Cuba. He had obtained it when he was there during the Spanish-American War.

But no one was hurt, and thanks be to God for that. The folks remained in Kitty Hawk until the next conference when Papa asked to be sent to Ocracoke — an island off the North Carolina coast. The people there were very wonderful to them and they were forever friends.

From Ocracoke I think they went to Bartow, Florida. Only Henry was at home with them then. After a year or so in Florida they moved back to the home Albert had bought for us in Bamberg, South Carolina. Papa never really retired, but filled in pastorates, did a lot of writing and gave counsel to many of the young ministers around who asked for it. He planted nineteen pecan trees on the place, along with peach trees, and corn, tomatoes, beans and peanuts. He even had one lovely magnolia tree in the front yard. The house and yard were enclosed by a white picket fence and Papa built a flagstone walk going from the front porch to the gate. This walk was made by broken pieces of granite from an old demolished cemetery! Only one piece had any marking on it, but the one at the front entrance read, "She is watching and waiting at the beautiful gate."

We had several family reunions at that home in Bamberg. By now we were scattered all over the country. Mama was the tie that kept us coming back. As I've stated so many times, we adored her. If ever she was ill, many of us would rush to her side to be sure she got the proper care.

I'll relate here one such instance which involved me. I wrote it as follows when I belonged to a creative writing class here in Plymouth, Michigan:

EMERGENCY JOURNEY

"He promised he'd call me if she ever got sick," I explained to my husband as I turned from answering the telephone.

It was midnight, and we had just gotten into the house, weary and worn, after spending a week in Chicago at a business convention.

The phone call was from my mother's physician in a tiny town in South Carolina. It seemed a long, long way from Michigan now. The doctor said to come at once, that she was very ill with pneumonia, and that at her age he didn't know how long she would last. I urged him to get her in the nearest hospital which was in a neighboring town. This he faithfully agreed to do.

"I think you'd better fly," my husband said, "even though I know you are terrified at the thought."

"Well," I replied, "I love her so much that maybe I won't be so scared of my own neck in my concern over her."

By the time we arrived at the airport in Detroit it was almost dawn and a cold misty rain was coming down. The lights about the area seemed detached and impersonal — as if they wouldn't bother to warm or welcome anyone or light your way to anywhere.

The man at the desk seemed tired and sleepy. "No, there isn't a regular flight right away, but there is an empty that is going to Cleveland in a few minutes to pick up some special passengers. You can take that."

So, shaking like a leaf and with that gone, empty feeling inside me, I stepped into the plane — the only passenger in the eighteen-place ship. As we took off, I waved a disconsolate good-bye to my husband. I could hardly distinguish his form in the wet mist.

Neither the pilot nor the copilot could have dreamed how terrified I was or one of them would surely have walked back to my seat to keep me company. As it was, during those forty-five minutes of flight, they just opened their door into the cockpit once in a while as if to see if I were still there. My hands gripped my purse like a vise all the way to Cleveland, and I sat straight and still, as if in the middle of a canoe.

The plane made a smooth landing, and I was able to get an immediate flight south. That plane was filled. I was the only woman passenger. Through the long day we droned through the sky, and I watched the calm, serene businessmen as they read their papers and sipped coffee. I was too squeamish for food or drink.

Just as I was beginning to relax a bit, the pilot announced, "We'll be landing in ten minutes. Fasten your seat belts please." The men folded their newspapers and began looking out the window. For fifty minutes no papers were reopened and yet no questions were asked. We kept circling the airport. When we finally landed and I was walking down the ramp, I timidly asked the pilot why we were so long. He answered, "Ceiling 300 feet. We had to wait for it to lift."

It was dark by this time — pitch dark. I took a cab to the hospital. Something told me to have the driver wait until I checked with the nurse at the desk. No, my mother hadn't been admitted! They knew nothing of her! Sick at heart, I knew that I was too late. Otherwise, the doctor would have had her here as he had promised.

I went back to the cab and asked the driver if he would take me to the town where mother lived. He said yes, but first he'd have to fill up the car with gas. When we drove up to the gas station he motioned to the attendant to speak to him in private. As they whispered to each other they would glance at me occasionally. What in the world . . . ?

However, when the tank was filled, the driver climbed behind the wheel and away we went.

As we got out of town, the driver suddenly turned off his headlights. Not a word of explanation to me, and I didn't ask any. I was frozen stiff with fear.

We drove along the highway — swamps along each side — a darkened farmhouse every mile or so. It seemed eons before we reached the familiar sign that read, "BAMBERG — POP. 2000." A block before we got to the house a state police car pulled alongside and the officer said, "Pull over." At the sight of him I began to feel a little bravery seeping into my veins. "Please," I said to him, "let me go home before you arrest him or whatever you are going to do." He got in with us and we drove on. I explained my situation to him, and, knowing my family, he asked to go in with me. Telling the cab driver to wait outside, he opened the door of our house and I practically fell in. The doctor and a nurse greeted us with the news that mother had responded beautifully to a new drug called sulfanilimide. It had not been necessary to hospitalize her.

Then, and only then, did I turn to the officer and ask, "What was wrong with that cab driver?"

"He was driving between towns without a license."

My father gladly paid his fine. As I kissed my mother a glad hello I said, "Well, for a little while I didn't know whether we'd greet each other in our earthly or our heavenly home today!"

As I wind down this saga, I must tell a few things about Sara first, and then Lil. I never knew of a single person who didn't love Sally — as we called her lots of times — or Sara Jane just for fun. She was cute and small, light and airy. Loved music and even was good at the violin for a while. All her life she enjoyed dancing. Her greatest fear was that she might be a burden to anybody and she lived her whole fifty-nine years making herself independent of us all. Whenever we got together, Sara was there — mostly momentarily, but happy and outgoing always, warmhearted and loving, but avoiding any deep involvement with us. She worked hard at her profession — medical records' secretary — and all the people she worked with adored her. She died very suddenly one day while at her office. When I went home for her funeral a strange thing happened to me. Tired after the long automobile trip from Michigan, I finally fell into bed and into a deep sleep. Suddenly I awoke and remembered a thing I had just dreamed; I saw Sara in a ballet outfit, dancing about a room and to my mind came the famous Wordsworth poem which I hadn't even heard for forty years — at least:

>   She was a phantom of delight
>   When first she gleamed upon my sight;
>   A lovely apparition, sent
>   To be a moment's ornament.

Indeed, to me, that was Sara.

Now about Lil — or Lillie as many of the family call her. She is "something else" — as the saying goes. When she took me under her wing she was like a fairy godmother from the very beginning. We went on beautiful trips together, up into Canada — Toronto, Montreal and Quebec — staying at the best hotels and seeing all the wonderful sights. She took me on trips on the big ships that travelled all the Great Lakes in those days. We spent some time on Mackinac Island. We visited Washington, D.C., and Shenandoah Valley with its Endless caverns. We took many a trip to visit Mama and Papa wherever they were living at the time. Finally, when I was eighteen, Lil said I might enter the University of Michigan School of Nursing. While I was there she saw that I got all the best advantages that were available at the university. There I heard all the leading artists in music who appeared at Hill Auditorium: Rachmaninoff, Fritz Kriesler, Rosa Ponselle, Lily Pons — all the concerts for all the years I was in Ann Arbor. Lil bought me the prettiest clothes and gave me a generous monthly allowance besides paying my tuition and all activity fees. In the meantime she visited me or had me visit her in Flint — about sixty miles away. The girls in the dorm used to say, "Your sister is here again with some beautiful clothes for you — darn it!"

In my senior year Lil had an accident in the operating room where she was assisting in a tonsillectomy. She ran a snare (tiny wire) through an index finger and got a strep infection of the tendon sheath. She was very, very sick for several weeks and almost lost her arm. I visited her as often as I could, but she insisted that I remain in school and study hard.

Just a couple of months after her hand had healed but was still very tender she drove over to Ann Arbor and brought me a perfectly gorgeous point d'esprit evening gown and a rosewood velvet reversible cape trimmed in a collar of white fur which she had made for me, all because I'd been invited to the J-Hop and she wanted me to look pretty! It was a cold, cold day, the first part of January, and she had skidded into a snowbank on the way to Ann Arbor!

Can you imagine what a kind of person *she* is?

She and the other girls in the family taught us younger ones some little "goodies" that I want to share with you.

Maybe lots of people know them, but home is the only place I ever heard them. Most of them were rhymes to say when "you were playing games when one would be 'it'."

> I went to the well to wash my toe
> And when I got back, my black-eyed chickie
> Was gone — O-U-T spells out and out you go
> With the old dirty dish rag tied around your neck!

or

> "My mama and your mama were out washing clothes.
> My mama hit your mama right smack on the nose.
> Did it hurt?" If the answer was Y E S, we'd say,
> "Y-E-S spells yes and out you go."

or

> Wire, briar, limber-lock
> Three geese in a flock.
> One flew east and
> One flew west and
> One flew over the cuckoo's nest.

A very few years ago most of us, with our husbands and children, met for a family reunion at the Hacienda on Lake Austin near Austin, Texas. That was wonderful — all of us under the same roof for the first time in ages! We sang the old songs for hours at a time, told tales about happenings at home, played bridge, went swimming, and drove around the countryside. One night the owners of the Hacienda invited all guests to a "you all come" on their paddle-wheel boat. It was a soft, moonlit night, but the stars were shining a-plenty. We brothers and sisters were standing together at the rail as we started down the river. Grace was beside me and in a quiet, sweet voice she quoted from Longfellow:

> Silently, one by one, in the infinite meadows
>   of heaven,
> Blossomed the lovely stars,
> The forget-me-nots of the angels.

I still get goose pimples when I remember that.

Several of Mama's and Papa's great-grandchildren were at the reunion there. One evening when the songfest and storytelling were almost over, Charles, one of the grandsons, picked up his little daughter Chris to take her to the car and back into town to their own home for the night. We were just beginning a final song when she said sleepily, "Take me back into the room, Daddy, the show has started again!"

Another summer (and we always had our reunion around and on August ninth because that was Mama's birthday) we gathered at The Carolinian at Nags Head, North Carolina — right on the Atlantic Ocean. Some friends of mine from here in Plymouth called at the inn the day we left, asking at the desk if there were any Bettses registered. The answer was, "My gracious! They're all over the place!"

At this point in our lives there are nine left. And so, to end this saga I shall quote a poem that Papa loved and that we sang often — to the tune of "Ingleside" (from *Songs of the University of North Carolina* — compiled by W. A. Betts, 1880).

The Home Eternal

> There's not a bright and beaming smile
> Which in this world I see,

But turns my heart to future joy
And whispers "Heaven" to me.
Though often here my soul is sad,
And falls the silent tear,
There is a world of smiles and love,
And sorrow dwells not there.

I never clasp a friendly hand
In greeting or farewell
But thoughts of my eternal home
Within by bosom swell.
There, where we meet with holy joy,
No thoughts of parting come.
But never ending ages still
Shall find us all at Home.